Color Funny Doodles
Colouring Book

'Book One: Humorous'

Hartmut Jager

My Fat Fox Ltd
MMXIV

My Fat Fox Ltd
86 Gladys Dimson House
London E7 9DF
United Kingdom
www.myfatfox.co.uk

Color Funny Doodles Colouring Book 1 Humorous
© 2014 Hartmut Jager

http://hartmut-jager.artistwebsites.com/

The rights of Hartmut Jager to be identified as the author of this work have been asserted by him in accordance with the Copyright, Designs and Patents Act, 1988

Cover design
© 2014 Hartmut Jager

http://hartmut-jager.artistwebsites.com/

ISBN 978-1-905747-38-2

Be Proud!

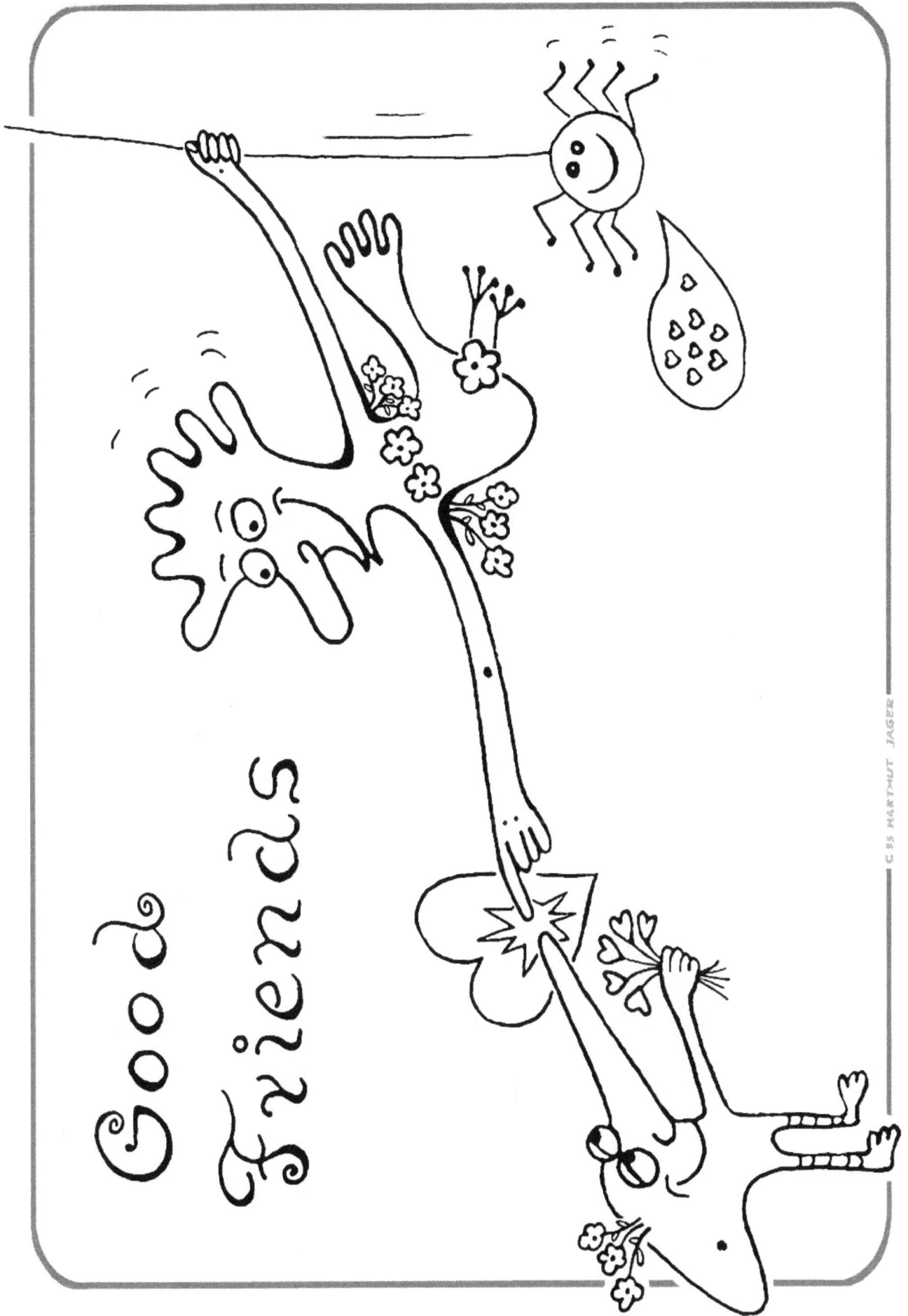

Good Friends

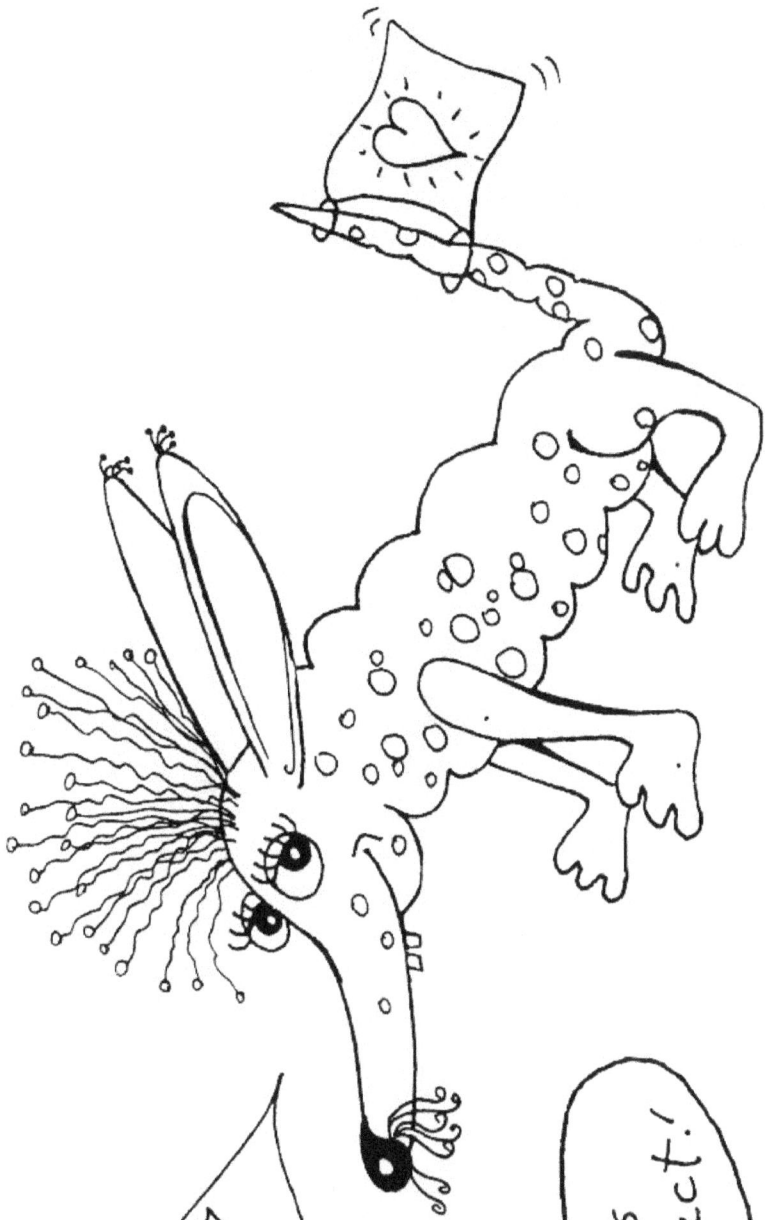

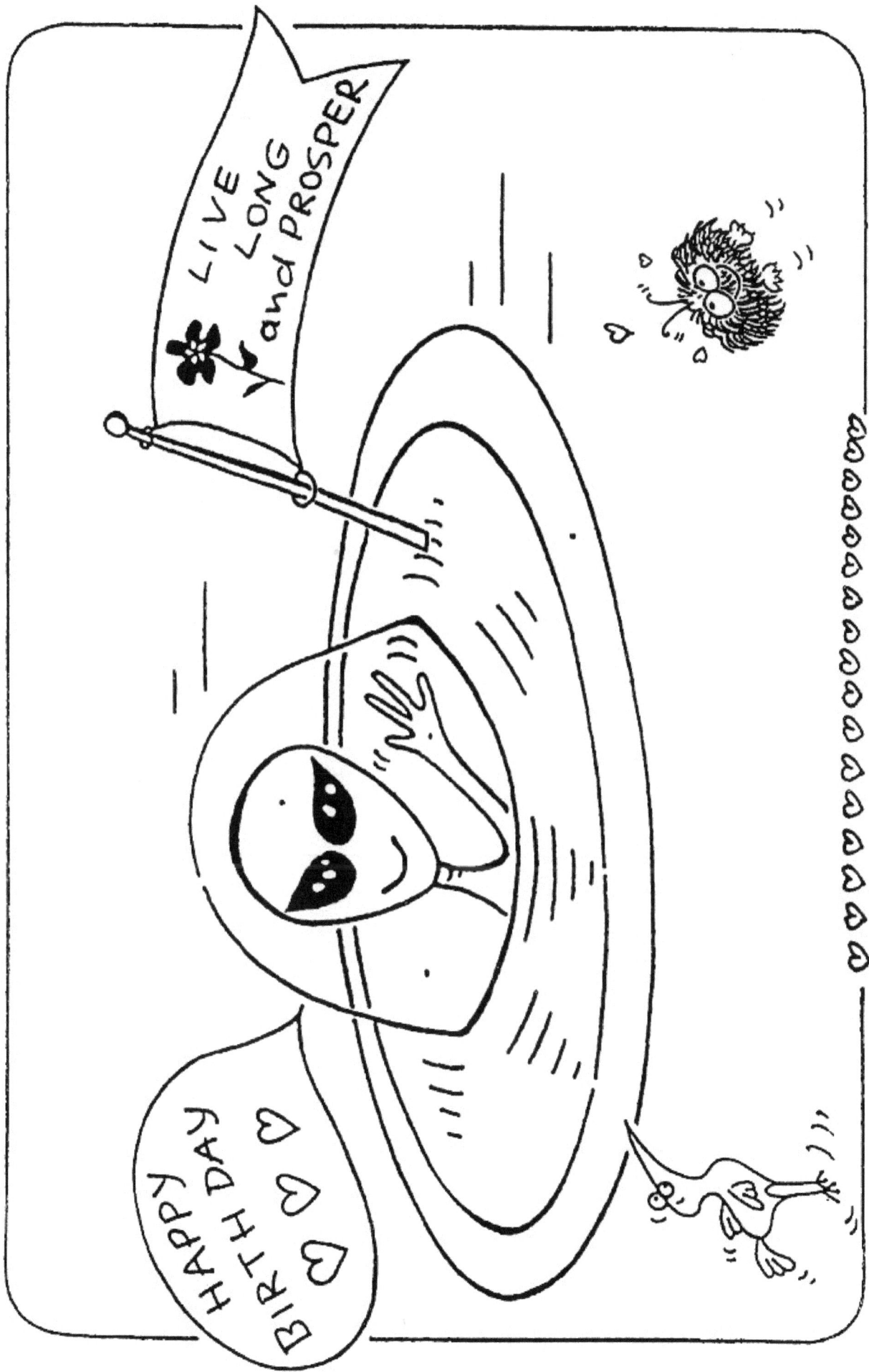

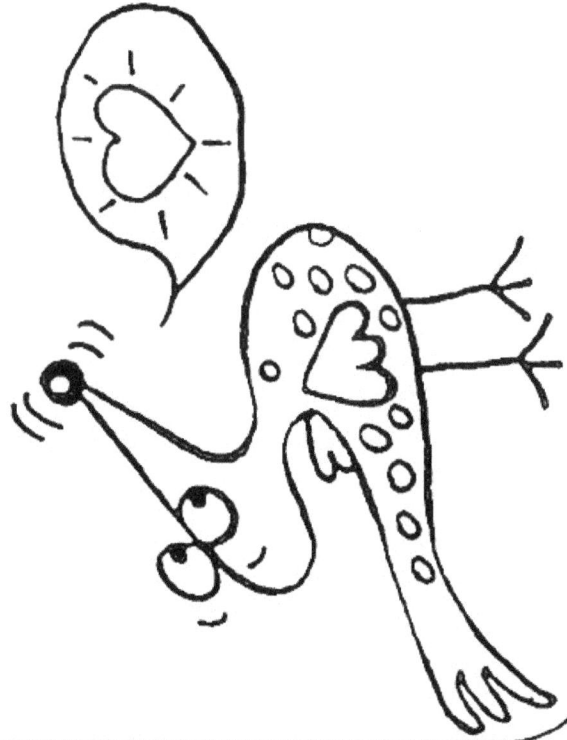

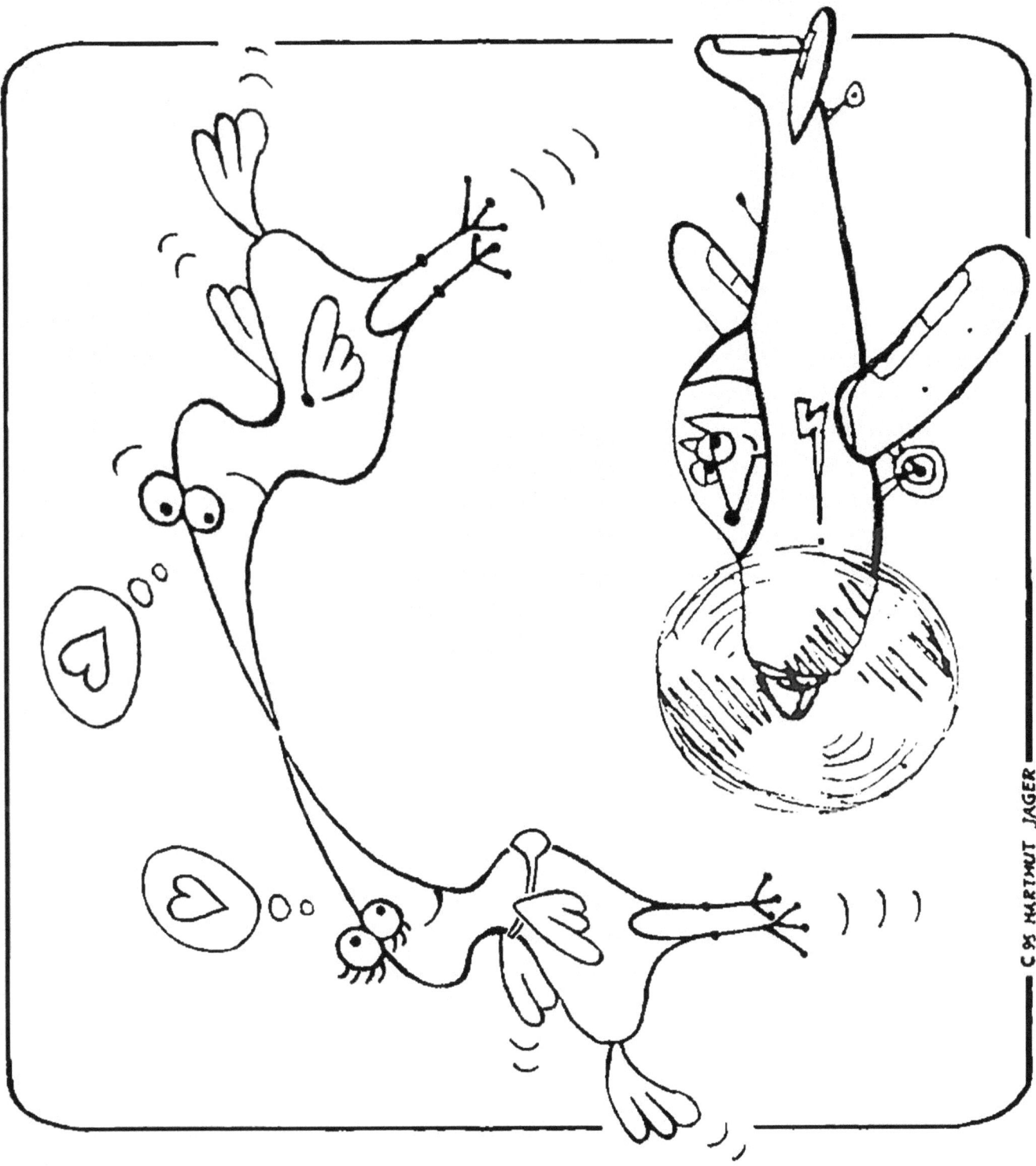

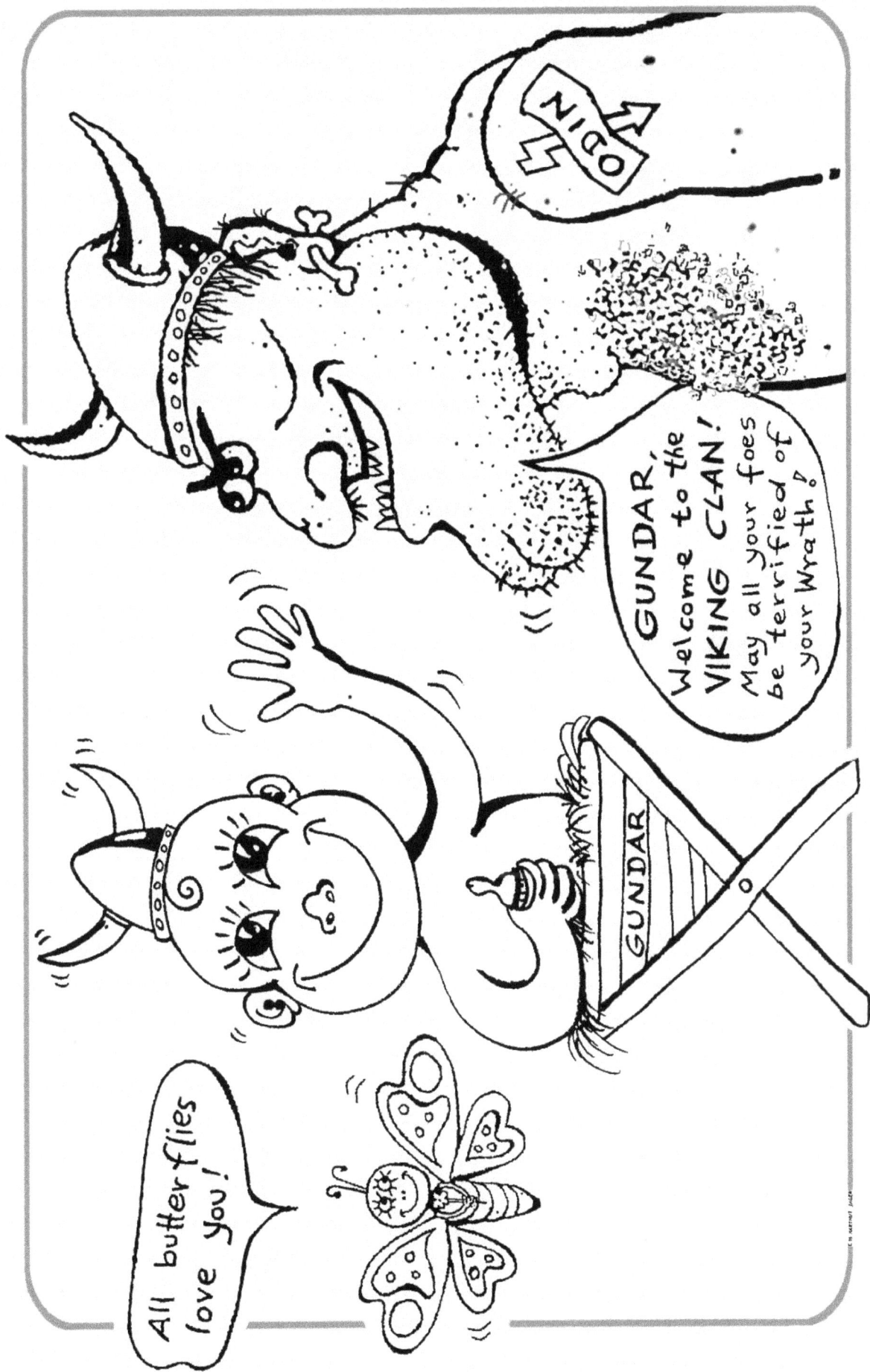

C 95 HARTMUT JAGER

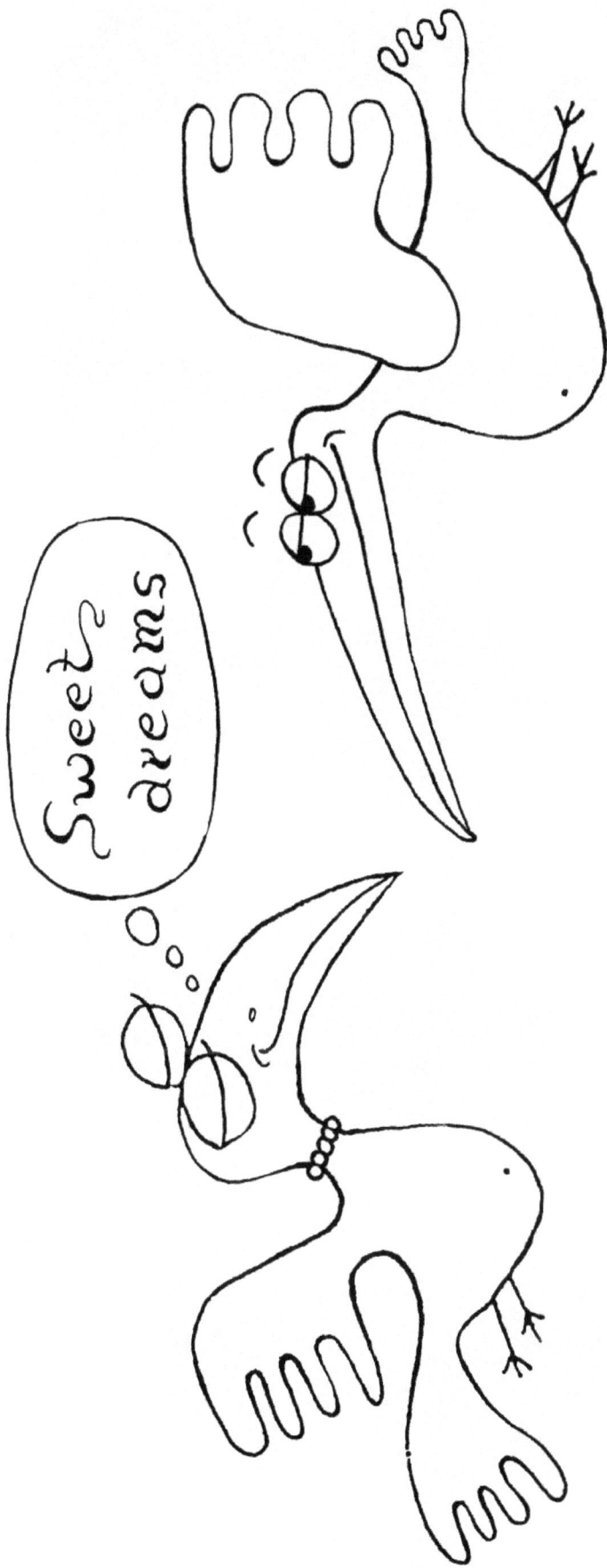

I'd like to steal
your heart
away
?

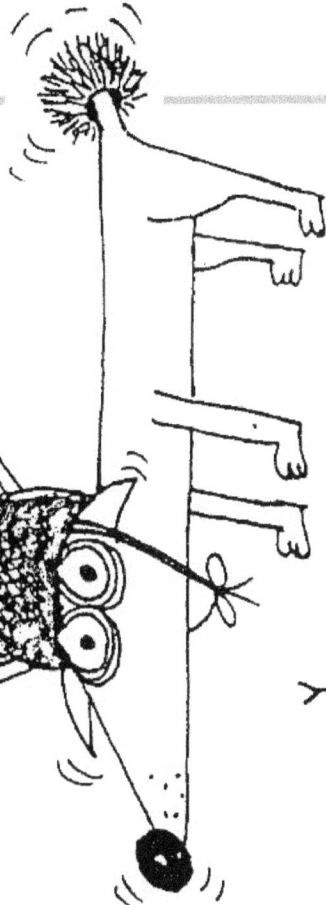

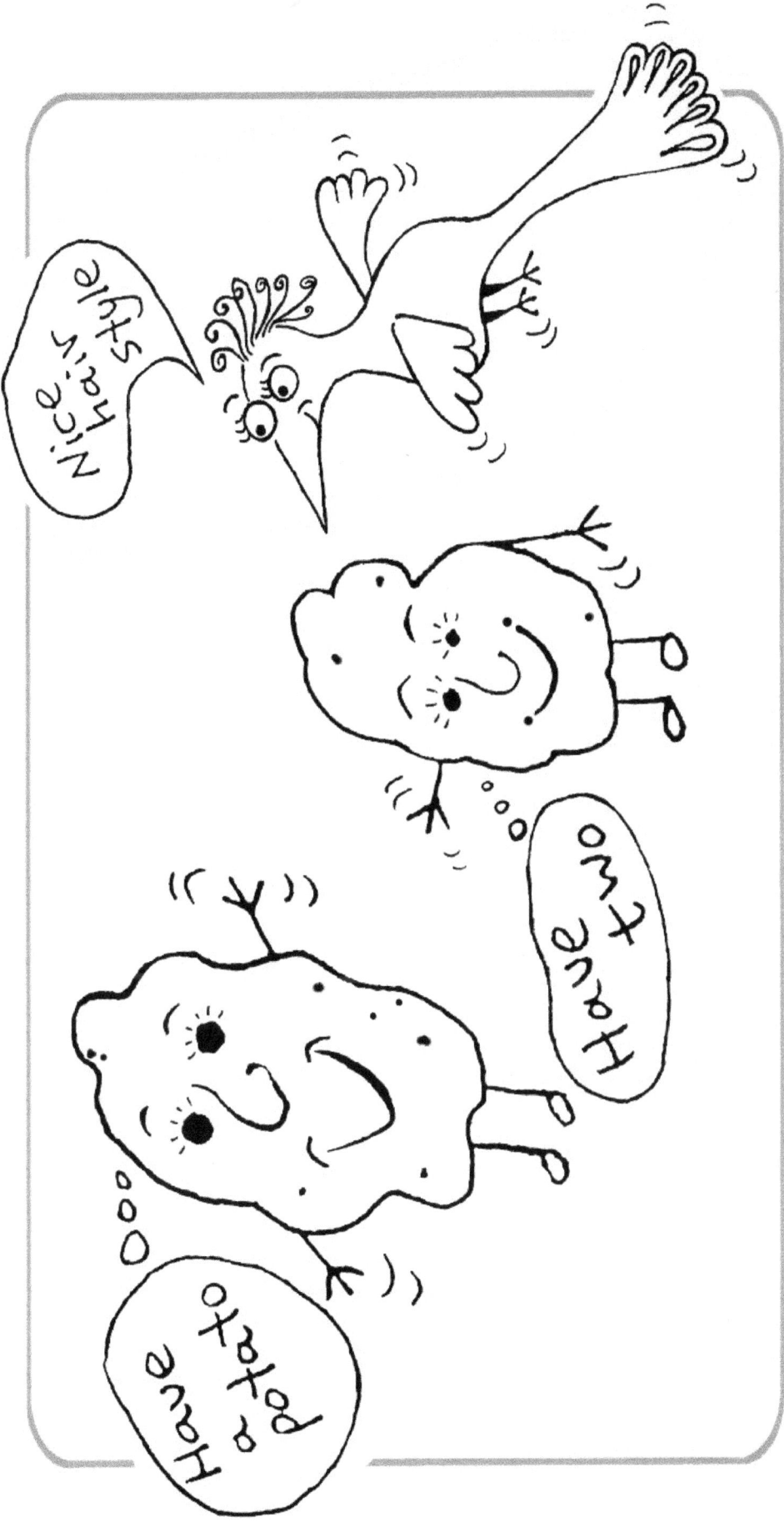

MaGic
I wish you lots

Have
Lots
of
xxx

I wish you lots of MAGIC

©95 hi

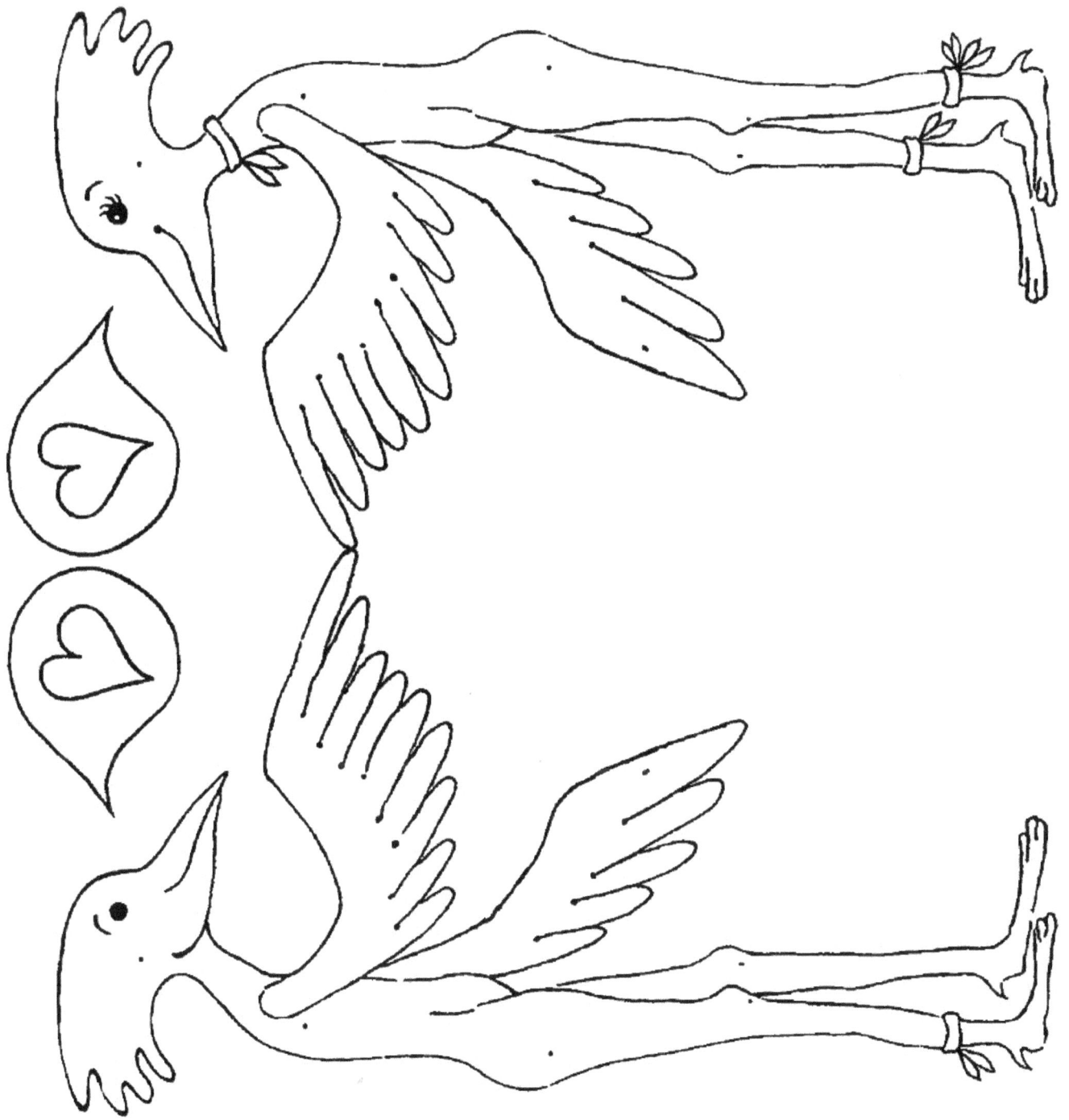

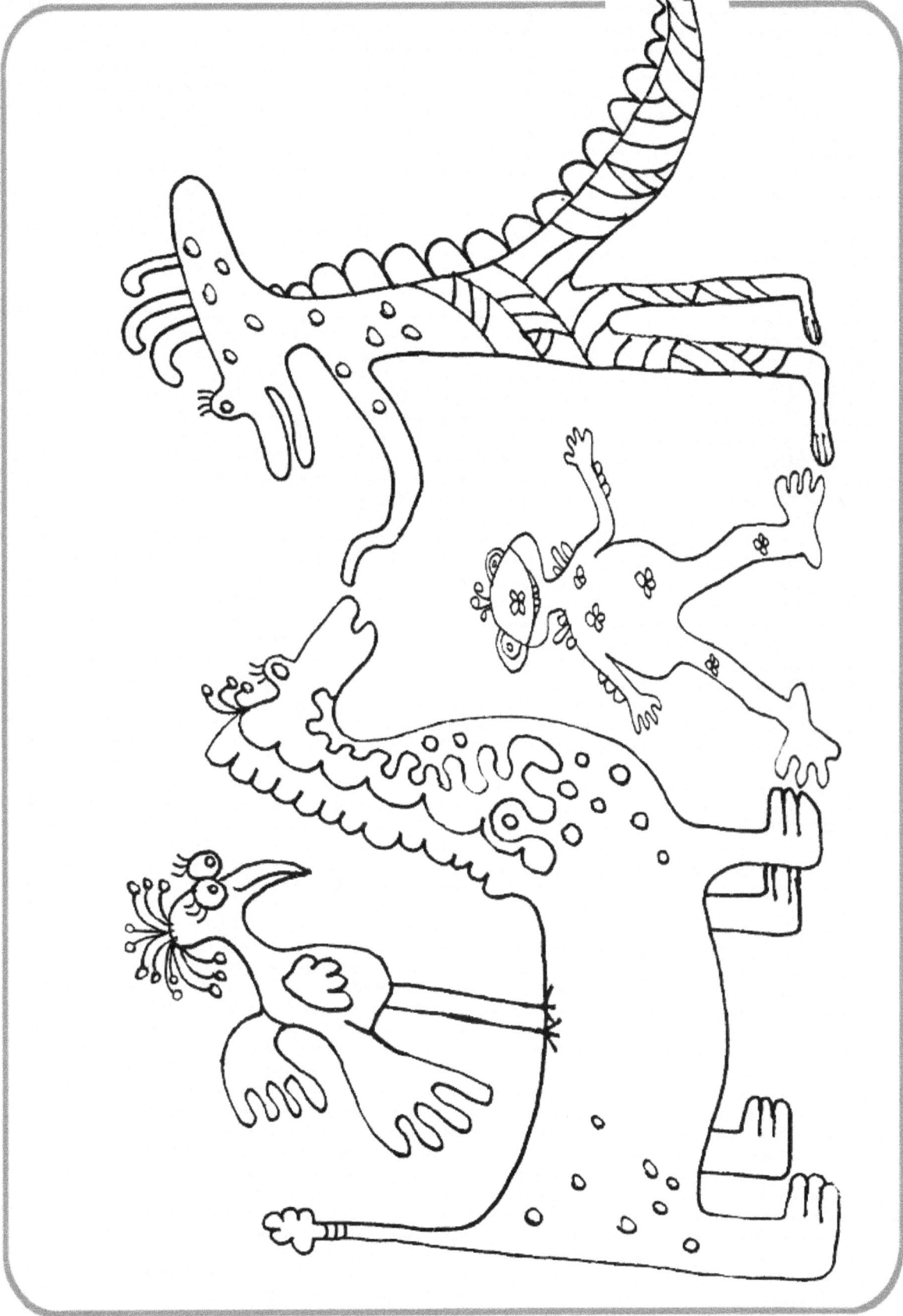

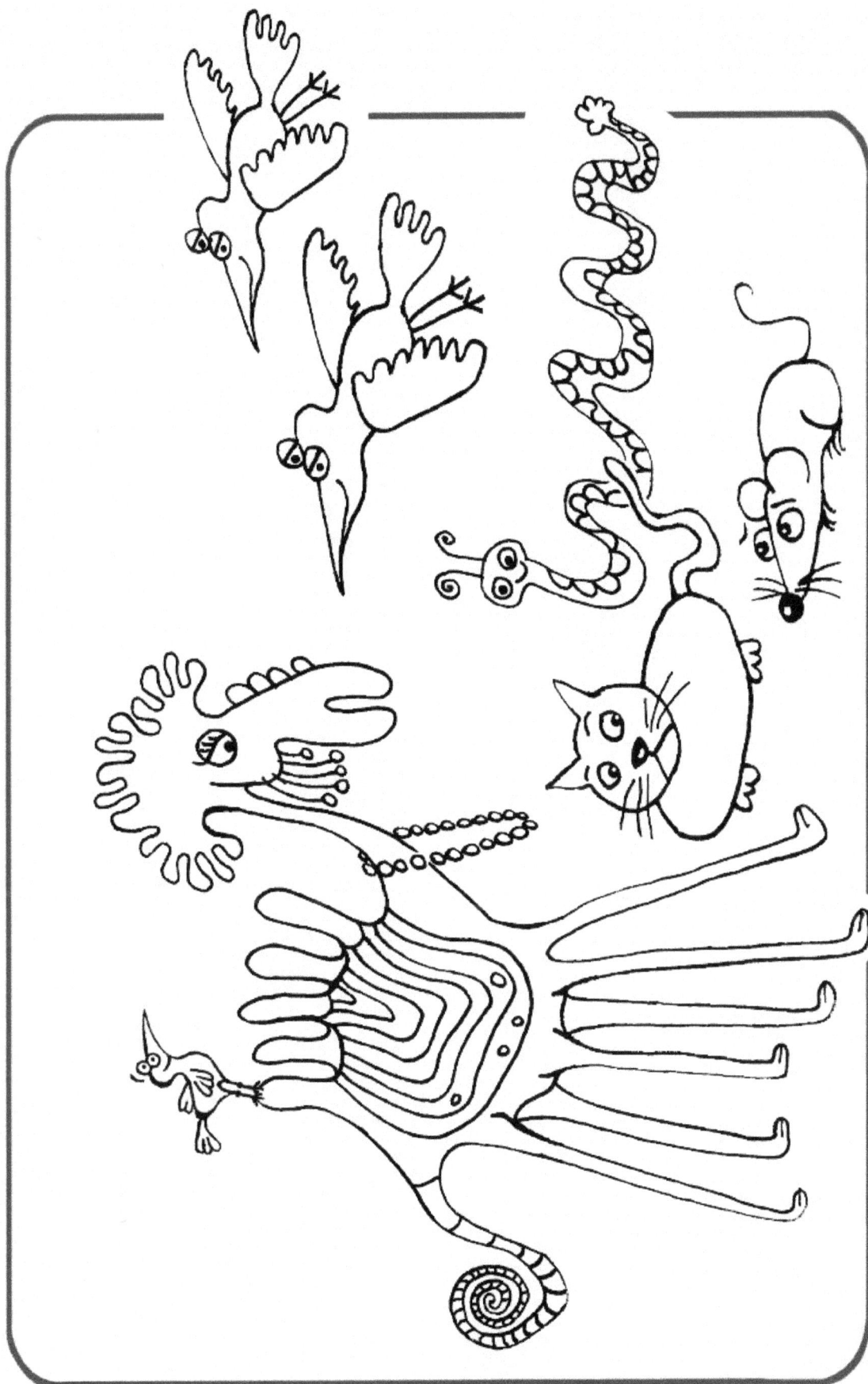

Be
Proud !

www.ingramcontent.com/pod-product-compliance
Lightning Source LLC
Chambersburg PA
CBHW081157090426
42736CB00017B/3365